CONTENTS

CHAPTER 1: Understanding Web 3.0

CHAPTER 2: From Web 1.0 to Web 3.0 – The Journey

CHAPTER 3: Key Components of Web 3

CHAPTER 4: Setting Up for Web 3: The Basics

CHAPTER 5: Web 3 Applications You Can Start Using Today

CHAPTER 6: A Step-by-Step Guide to Investing in Web 3

CHAPTER 7: How to Stay Safe in the Web 3 World

CHAPTER 8: The Emerging Phase of Web 3

CONCLUSION: Your First Steps in Web 3

DISCLAIMER

NOTES

INTRODUCTION

The internet has revolutionized our lives in ways that were unimaginable just a few decades ago. From the early, static websites of the 1990s to the interactive social media platforms we use today, the web has evolved rapidly. Now, we are on the brink of another significant transformation—the emergence of Web 3 a decentralized version of the internet that seeks to give control back to users.

While Web 3 may sound complicated at first, its foundation is built on a simple premise: ownership Unlike the centralized platforms of Web 2.0 (like Google, Facebook, and Twitter), where a handful of companies control your data, Web 3 is powered by blockchain technology, allowing users to take full control of their online presence, digital assets, and interactions. In this new era, you are not just a passive user but an active participant who owns their data and identity.

You might have come across terms like blockchain, cryptocurrency, NFTs, and DeFi and felt overwhelmed by the technical jargon. Don't worry—this book will break down these concepts in a simple, easy-to-understand way, guiding you step by step into the world of Web 3. Whether

you're looking to explore cryptocurrencies, acquire digital assets, or dive into decentralized apps (dApps), this guide is here to help you get started.

Why Web 3 is Important

The shift from Web 1.0 to Web 2.0 introduced an interactive internet where users could both consume and create content through blogs, social media, and forums. However, this also led to the rise of a few powerful platforms controlling vast amounts of user data, dictating what we see, share, and how we engage online. Concerns about data privacy, censorship, and the dominance of tech giants have grown over time.

Web 3 addresses these challenges by creating a decentralized internet Built on blockchain technology, Web 3 enables transactions and interactions between users without the need for intermediaries like tech companies. Instead of centralized authorities, trust is established through smart contracts and decentralized networks. The potential of Web 3 is vast, with the power to reshape industries such as finance, entertainment, and digital ownership.

What You'll Discover in This Book

This ebook is designed to make Web 3 easy to understand and accessible to everyone. We'll guide you through the essential concepts and tools needed to explore this new space, from setting up a crypto wallet and acquiring cryptocurrency to interacting with decentralized apps (dApps). You'll learn about key technologies such as blockchain NFTs, and DAOs, and understand how they work and why they matter.

By the end of this book, you'll know how to:

- Grasp the evolution of the internet from Web 1.0 to Web 3.0.

- Set up and protect your own cryptocurrency wallet.

- Purchase and securely store digital currencies like Bitcoin and Ethereum.

- Use decentralized apps and navigate Web 3 platforms.

- Explore investment opportunities through DeFi, NFTs, and

DAOs.

- Identify risks and follow best practices for security in Web 3.

Web 3 is more than just technology it's a reimagining of how the internet operates, giving users true ownership and control. Whether you're new to the idea of decentralized finance, curious about NFTs, or want to learn more about digital privacy, this book will provide you with a straightforward guide to entering the Web 3 world.

As you take these first steps into Web 3, keep in mind that the space is constantly evolving. Learning about it now will put you ahead of the curve as this new, decentralized internet continues to grow. The possibilities are endless, and your journey into Web 3 starts here.

CHAPTER 1

UNDERSTANDING WEB 3

In just a few decades, the internet has gone through dramatic shifts, shaping the way we interact, conduct business, and entertain ourselves. Web 1.0, often called the "static web," was the earliest form of the internet. It was essentially a collection of read-only pages, with minimal interaction between users and the web. Websites were basic, with simple text, few images, and little user-generated content.

Web 2.0, also known as the "social web," took the internet to a new level by enabling users to interact and share information more freely. It birthed platforms like Facebook, YouTube, and Twitter, where content was created not just by companies but also by everyday users. However, the rise of big tech monopolies has also centralized control over the internet, leading to concerns about privacy, censorship, and data ownership.

Enter Web 3.0, the next iteration of the web, which promises to decentralize power and give control back to users. At its core, Web 3 is built on blockchain technology a distributed ledger system that ensures transparency and security. The key idea is decentralization: no single entity owns the web, and users have more control over their data, identity, and online assets.

In this ebook, you will learn everything you need to know to get started with Web 3. We will explore the evolution of the internet, the technologies driving Web 3, and practical steps for diving into this new world. Whether you're a complete beginner or someone who wants to deepen your understanding, this guide is designed

JUZZY ISAIAH

to be your starting point for everything Web 3.

CHAPTER 2

FROM WEB 1.0 TO WEB3.0 THE JOURNEY

The internet has been evolving continuously, but it can be helpful to break down its growth into three key phases: Web 1.0, Web 2.0, and now Web 3.0.

Web 1.0 (The Static Web): The early 1990s saw the birth of the web. It was primarily informational, with no interactivity. Think of Web 1.0 as a vast library where you could only read, but not engage. There were no comment sections, social media platforms, or dynamic websites.

Web 2.0 (The Social Web): Starting in the early 2000s, Web 2.0 introduced user-generated content, making the internet more interactive. Blogs, social media, and cloud-based apps emerged. With this new freedom, however, came the concentration of power in the hands of a few companies, like Google and Facebook.

Web 3.0 (The Decentralized Web): As a response to the over-centralization of Web 2.0, Web 3 introduces a decentralized structure where users can truly own their data. At its heart, Web 3 is powered by blockchain technology, cryptocurrency, and smart contracts, which allow for peer-to-peer transactions without needing an intermediary.

These three phases represent the ongoing transformation of the web. While Web 2.0 opened up the possibilities for interaction, Web 3.0 is changing who holds the keys to control and ownership online.

CHAPTER 3

KEY COMPONENTS OF WEB 3

Understanding the foundational technologies that make Web 3 possible is crucial for any newbie. Below, we'll break down the major components:

Blockchain Technology: A distributed, digital ledger system where transactions are recorded in a secure and transparent manner. Think of it as an open book of accounts that's maintained by everyone involved, preventing fraud or tampering.

Cryptocurrencies: Digital or virtual tokens that rely on blockchain technology. Bitcoin, Ethereum, and countless others fuel transactions in the Web 3 ecosystem.

Smart Contracts: These are self-executing contracts with the terms of the agreement directly written into code. Smart contracts eliminate the need for intermediaries like banks or lawyers.

Decentralized Autonomous Organizations (DAOs): Organizations governed by code rather than people, where decisions are made by token holders through a voting system.

NFTs (Non-Fungible Tokens): These are unique digital assets that represent ownership of art, music, virtual goods, and more. Unlike cryptocurrencies, each NFT is distinct.

CHAPTER 4

SETTING UP FOR WEB 3.0 THE BASICS

Before diving into the world of Web 3 applications, there are a few essentials that you need to set up. The Web 3 ecosystem relies heavily on blockchain technology, and to interact with it, you'll need a crypto wallet and access to cryptocurrencies. In this chapter, we'll walk through the step-by-step process to get you started.

1. What is a Crypto Wallet?

A crypto wallet is your entry point into Web 3. It's similar to an account or an app that lets you store, send, and receive cryptocurrencies. But unlike traditional bank accounts, a crypto wallet allows you to hold full control of your assets.

There are two main types of wallets:

Custodial Wallets: These wallets are held by a third party, such as a cryptocurrency exchange (e.g., Binance, Coinbase). You don't control the private keys, meaning you're trusting a third party to keep your funds safe. This is typically the easiest way to get started.

Non-Custodial Wallets: These wallets allow you to fully own your private keys and, in turn, your crypto assets. Popular options include MetaMask, Trust Wallet, and Ledger hardware wallets. It provides more control but also requires more responsibility in securing your funds.

2. Setting Up a Crypto Wallet: Step-by-Step

Let's walk through setting up a basic, non-custodial wallet (e.g.,

MetaMask) for Web 3 use:

Download MetaMask: Available as a browser extension or mobile app, MetaMask is one of the most popular wallets for interacting with Web 3 applications. Visit metamask.io to download it.

Create a Wallet: Once installed, you'll be prompted to create a new wallet. Follow the instructions to set up a secure password.

Backup Your Seed Phrase: MetaMask (and all non-custodial wallets) will provide you with a "seed phrase" — a series of 12-24 words that acts as a backup to access your wallet. This phrase is your lifeline. If you lose it, you lose access to your funds forever. Write it down and store it safely offline.

Wallet Setup Complete: Once your seed phrase is safely stored and your wallet is created, you're ready to start using MetaMask.

3. Securing Your Wallet: Best Practices

Since Web 3 involves managing your own assets, security is paramount. Here are a few best practices for keeping your wallet safe:

Enable Two-Factor Authentication (2FA): If your wallet or exchange offers 2FA, always enable it for extra security.

Use a Hardware Wallet: For long-term storage of large amounts of crypto, hardware wallets like Ledger or Trezor provide an extra layer of security by keeping your private keys offline.

Never Share Your Seed Phrase: No legitimate platform or person will ever ask for your seed phrase. Keep it private, as sharing it gives others full access to your wallet.

4. Acquiring Cryptocurrency: Step-by-Step

Now that you've set up a wallet, the next step is to acquire some cryptocurrency. You'll need crypto to participate in most Web 3 applications.

Choose a Crypto Exchange: Popular exchanges for beginners include Coinbase, Binance, and Kraken. These platforms allow you to exchange fiat currency (USD, EUR, etc.) for cryptocurrencies like Bitcoin, Ethereum, and others.

Create an Account: Sign up for an account on your chosen exchange. You'll need to go through some verification processes, such as providing a government-issued ID.

Deposit Funds: Once your account is verified, you can deposit fiat currency using a bank transfer, credit card, or other payment methods offered by the exchange.

Buy Cryptocurrency: After your funds are deposited, use the exchange to purchase your desired cryptocurrency (e.g., Ethereum). Ethereum is widely used in Web 3 apps, so it's a good starting point.

Transfer Crypto to Your Wallet: Once you've acquired cryptocurrency, transfer it from the exchange to your MetaMask wallet for safekeeping. Exchanges can be hacked, and it's safer to store your crypto in a private wallet.

5. Navigating Gas Fees and Transaction Costs

One important concept in Web 3 is 'gas fees' the cost of processing transactions on a blockchain. These fees are paid to miners or validators who secure the network. On Ethereum, gas fees can vary depending on the network's congestion.

How to Manage Gas Fees: MetaMask and most wallets will estimate the gas fees before you send a transaction. It's wise to avoid times of high network congestion to minimize costs.

Alternatives: If Ethereum's gas fees are too high, consider using layer 2 solutions like Polygon or alternative blockchains like Binance Smart Chain (BSC), which offer lower transaction costs.

CHAPTER 5

WEB 3 APPLICATIONS YOU CAN START USING TODAY

Once your wallet is set up and funded, you're ready to start exploring Web 3 applications. In this chapter, we'll introduce several Web 3 use cases and platforms you can dive into right away.

1. Decentralized Finance (DeFi)

DeFi is one of the biggest innovations in Web 3, allowing anyone to borrow, lend, and earn interest without intermediaries like banks.

What is DeFi?

DeFi stands for decentralized finance. It replaces traditional financial institutions with smart contracts running on blockchains. Instead of applying for a loan from a bank, you can lend or borrow assets directly from other users.

Popular DeFi Apps:

Uniswap: A decentralized exchange (DEX) for swapping cryptocurrencies.

Aave: A lending platform that lets you earn interest or borrow assets.

Compound: Another popular DeFi app for lending and borrowing.

How to Get Started with DeFi:

Go to the DeFi app (e.g., Uniswap) and connect your MetaMask wallet.

Deposit cryptocurrency into the platform.

Follow the app's instructions to lend, borrow, or swap tokens.

2. Decentralized Apps (dApps)

Decentralized apps (dApps) are applications that run on blockchain networks instead of centralized servers. Unlike traditional apps, dApps can offer greater transparency and user control.

Popular dApps:

MetaMask: As discussed earlier, MetaMask is a Web 3 wallet, but it also acts as a gateway to many decentralized apps.

Brave Browser: A privacy-focused browser that rewards users with Basic Attention Tokens (BAT) for viewing ads.

3. Play-to-Earn Gaming

The gaming world is being transformed by Web 3 through play-to-earn games, where users can earn real value (in the form of cryptocurrencies or NFTs) by playing.

Popular Games:

Axie Infinity: A digital pet universe where players breed and battle creatures called Axies, earning tokens that can be traded for real money.

The Sandbox: A virtual world where players can own land, build experiences, and trade NFTs.

How to Get Started:

- Create an account on the gaming platform.
- Connect your crypto wallet (e.g., MetaMask).
- Start playing to earn tokens or assets that can be traded on the platform's marketplace.

4. Exploring the Metaverse

The metaverse is a virtual world where users can socialize, trade, and own digital assets. In Web 3, the metaverse is decentralized, allowing users to truly own virtual land and items.

Popular Metaverse Platforms:

Decentraland: A 3D virtual world where users can buy land, create experiences, and interact with others.

Cryptovoxels: Another virtual world focused on creativity,

allowing users to build structures, art, and games.
How to Get Started:
- Sign up on the metaverse platform.
- Purchase land or assets using cryptocurrency.
- Start exploring or building your virtual presence.

CHAPTER 6

A STEP-BY-STEP GUIDE TO INVESTING IN WEB 3

Investing in Web 3 is an exciting opportunity, but it requires careful research and understanding. In this chapter, we'll cover how to navigate the investment landscape in Web 3 safely.

1. Researching Web 3 Projects

Before investing in any Web 3 project, it's essential to do thorough research. Some key things to look for include:

The Team: Check the background and credibility of the project founders.

The Technology: Understand the problem the project is solving and the technology behind it.

The Community: A strong, active community is a good sign of a project's potential.

The Tokenomics: Review how the project's token is structured, its supply, and its utility within the ecosystem.

2. Participating in ICOs (Initial Coin Offerings)

ICOs are a way for Web 3 projects to raise funds by selling tokens to early investors. While they offer high rewards, they can also be high-risk.

3. How to Buy Tokens and Participate in ICOs

Participating in an ICO (Initial Coin Offering) allows you to invest in new Web 3 projects at an early stage. Here's a step-by-step guide to getting involved:

Research the ICO: Make sure to thoroughly vet the project by reading its whitepaper, checking the team behind it, and verifying its use case and roadmap.

Create a Wallet: Most ICOs require you to have a compatible wallet, such as MetaMask or Trust Wallet, where you can receive tokens. Ensure your wallet supports the token standard (e.g., ERC-20 for Ethereum-based projects).

Acquire the Required Cryptocurrency: ICOs usually accept major cryptocurrencies like Ethereum or Bitcoin. You'll need to have these coins in your wallet to participate.

Register for the ICO: Follow the registration process on the ICO's official website, which may involve providing your wallet address and completing Know Your Customer (KYC) verification.

Participate in the ICO: Once the ICO opens, send your cryptocurrency to the project's wallet address, as specified. In return, you'll receive the new token, which will appear in your wallet.

Stay Updated: Follow the project's updates and community channels (e.g., Discord, Twitter) to stay informed on token listings, developments, and potential token price movements.

4. Understanding Market Volatility and Managing Risk

Web 3 investments, particularly cryptocurrencies, are highly volatile. Prices can swing dramatically in short periods. Managing risk is key:

Diversify Your Portfolio: Don't put all your funds into one project or token. Spread your investments across different sectors, such as DeFi, NFTs, and gaming tokens.

Set Realistic Expectations: While Web 3 offers high-reward opportunities, it also comes
with high risks. Avoid the temptation to chase quick profits.

Use Stop-Loss Orders: On exchanges, you can set stop-loss orders to automatically sell an asset if its price falls below a certain threshold, helping to limit losses.

Only Invest What You Can Afford to Lose: Never invest money you can't afford to lose. This is a golden rule in the volatile world of cryptocurrency and Web 3.

5. Earning Passive Income in Web 3

Aside from trading and holding tokens, you can also earn passive income through various Web 3 mechanisms:

Staking: Locking your tokens in a blockchain network to help secure it in return for rewards. Popular networks like Ethereum (once it fully transitions to Ethereum 2.0) and Polkadot offer staking rewards.

Yield Farming: Providing liquidity to decentralized finance (DeFi) platforms in exchange for interest or additional tokens. Yield farming can be done on platforms like Aave, Compound, or Uniswap.

Lending: Similar to traditional finance, you can lend out your cryptocurrency on DeFi platforms and earn interest on your assets. Platforms like Aave and Compound allow users to lend and borrow assets without intermediaries.

6. Staying Updated on Web 3 Trends

Web 3 is fast-evolving, and keeping up with the latest trends and developments is essential for success. Here are some key resources:

News Platforms: CoinDesk, CoinTelegraph, and The Block provide regular updates on the blockchain and crypto industry.

YouTube Channels and Podcasts: Channels like "Bankless" and "Coin Bureau" offer deep dives into Web 3 projects and tutorials.

Community Forums: Reddit communities such as Crypto Currency and Twitter (also known as "Crypto Twitter") are great for staying in the loop on Web 3 trends.

GitHub and Whitepapers: For more technical details, GitHub repositories and whitepapers of projects can provide insights into a project's codebase and vision.

CHAPTER 7

HOW TO STAY SAFE IN THE WEB 3 WORLD

As exciting as Web 3 is, the decentralized nature of the space also opens doors for scams, hacks, and phishing attempts. In this chapter, we'll explore best practices to stay safe and protect your assets in the Web 3 ecosystem.

1. Common Web 3 Scams and How to Avoid Them

Phishing Scams: These involve attackers tricking you into providing your private keys or seed phrase. Always ensure you're interacting with legitimate websites by double-checking URLs and never sharing your private keys.

Rug Pulls: In Web 3, a rug pull happens when developers abandon a project and run off with investor funds. Avoid rug pulls by researching projects thoroughly, especially new DeFi platforms, and look for signs of a genuine, long-term team.

Fake Airdrops: Be cautious of offers for "free tokens" in exchange for providing personal information or crypto. Always verify the legitimacy of the airdrop.

2. Recognizing Phishing Attempts and Fraud

To spot phishing attempts:

Check URLs: Ensure the website URL is correct, and avoid clicking links from unknown sources.

Watch for Fake Social Media Accounts: Scammers often impersonate known figures or projects. Always cross-check official social media pages.

Enable Wallet Notifications: Platforms like MetaMask can send alerts for unusual transactions. Enable these to keep an eye on activity.

3. Protecting Your Private Keys and Passwords

Use Cold Storage: Store large amounts of cryptocurrency in hardware wallets (cold storage), which are disconnected from the internet and less vulnerable to hacks.

Secure Your Seed Phrase: Write down your seed phrase on paper and store it in a secure location. Avoid saving it digitally, as online storage can be vulnerable to attacks.

4. Regulatory Concerns and How to Navigate Them

Regulation in the Web 3 space is still evolving. Different countries have varying rules around cryptocurrency, ICOs, and digital assets. As you engage with Web 3, it's important to:

Stay Informed on Local Regulations: Some countries require taxes on cryptocurrency gains, while others have restrictions on ICOs. Make sure to comply with local laws.

Be Wary of Anonymity Issues: While Web 3 emphasizes user control, governments are increasingly imposing regulations around KYC (Know Your Customer) and AML (Anti-Money Laundering) measures. Be prepared to share information when interacting with regulated platforms.

CHAPTER 8

THE EMERGING PHASE OF WEB 3

Web 3 is still in its infancy, but its potential is vast. In this chapter, we explore what the future may hold for this decentralized internet and the opportunities it presents.

1. The Impact on Industries
Web 3 has the potential to transform various industries:
Finance: DeFi and cryptocurrency will continue to disrupt traditional banking systems by offering more accessible, efficient alternatives.
Healthcare: Blockchain technology could enable secure, decentralized medical records and more transparent pharmaceutical supply chains.
Entertainment: NFTs and Web 3 will allow creators to maintain more control over their work and monetize their creations without the need for intermediaries.
Gaming and Virtual Realities: The rise of play-to-earn games and metaverse platforms will transform how we interact with digital worlds, blending entertainment, work, and economics.

2. Privacy, Identity, and Ownership in Web 3
Web 3 is fundamentally changing how we think about privacy, identity, and ownership online:
Privacy: Blockchain allows for encrypted, pseudonymous transactions, giving users more control over their data.
Self-Sovereign Identity: Web 3 enables users to own their

digital identity, independent of corporations or governments, and selectively share information.

Ownership: With NFTs and decentralized protocols, users can truly own digital assets—whether they are in-game items, art, or even pieces of the internet itself.

3. Regulatory Responses and Challenges

As Web 3 grows, governments and regulators will continue to grapple with how to monitor and regulate this new digital frontier. The challenge will be balancing innovation with the need for consumer protection and security.

Decentralization vs. Regulation: The decentralized nature of Web 3 is at odds with traditional regulatory frameworks, and finding middle ground will be crucial.

Global Standards: Countries will need to collaborate on creating global standards for regulating Web 3 technologies, as the internet knows no borders.

4. Predictions for the Next Decade

Mass Adoption: Web 3 technologies like DeFi, NFTs, and DAOs will become more mainstream as user interfaces improve and regulatory clarity increases.

Interoperability: Blockchains will become more interconnected, allowing assets and data to flow seamlessly across different networks.

New Business Models: Web 3 will create new business models that we haven't even thought of yet, just as Web 2.0 gave rise to gig economy platforms like Uber and Airbnb.

CONCLUSION

YOUR FIRST STEPS IN WEB 3

Congratulations! You've now been introduced to the basics of Web 3. As a newbie, you've learned about the history of the web, how blockchain and cryptocurrencies are reshaping the digital landscape, and how to get started with tools like crypto wallets and decentralized apps. Here's a quick recap of your next steps: Set Up a Wallet: If you haven't already, download a wallet like MetaMask and secure your seed phrase. Acquire Cryptocurrency: Use a trusted exchange to buy crypto, and transfer it to your wallet. Explore Web 3 Apps: Start with simple applications like DeFi platforms or play-to-earn games. Invest Wisely: Research Web 3 projects thoroughly before investing, and only invest what you can afford to lose. Stay Informed and Safe: Follow Web 3 news, and always prioritize security when dealing with your assets. Web 3 offers a world of opportunities, and the potential for growth and innovation is immense. The more you explore, the more comfortable you will become in this new digital frontier. Your journey into Web 3 is just beginning, and there's so much more to learn and discover. So, take your first steps today and be part of the future of the internet.

DISCLAIMER

This book was written using artificial intelligence (AI). While efforts were made by me to ensure accuracy, the content is for informational and educational purposes only.

The author and AI tools do not guarantee its completeness or accuracy and are not liable for errors. Readers should independently verify any information.

Thanks for reading.

JUZZY ISAIAH

www.ingramcontent.com/pod-product-compliance
Lightning Source LLC
Chambersburg PA
CBHW071003220526
45471CB00007B/3148